Best Inventions

Telephone

by Julie Murray

Dash!
LEVELED READERS
An Imprint of Abdo Zoom • abdobooks.com

Dash!
LEVELED READERS

Level 1 – Beginning
Short and simple sentences with familiar words or patterns for children who are beginning to understand how letters and sounds go together.

Level 2 – Emerging
Longer words and sentences with more complex language patterns for readers who are practicing common words and letter sounds.

Level 3 – Transitional
More developed language and vocabulary for readers who are becoming more independent.

THIS BOOK CONTAINS RECYCLED MATERIALS

abdobooks.com

Published by Abdo Zoom, a division of ABDO, PO Box 398166, Minneapolis, Minnesota 55439.

Printed in the United States of America, North Mankato, Minnesota.
102022
012023

Photo Credits: Getty Images, Shutterstock
Production Contributors: Kenny Abdo, Jennie Forsberg, Grace Hansen, John Hansen
Design Contributors: Candice Keimig, Neil Klinepier, Colleen McLaren

Library of Congress Control Number: 2022937319

Publisher's Cataloging in Publication Data

Names: Murray, Julie, author.
Title: Telephone / by Julie Murray
Description: Minneapolis, Minnesota : Abdo Zoom, 2023 | Series: Best inventions | Includes online resources and index.
Identifiers: ISBN 9781098280192 (lib. bdg.) | ISBN 9781098280727 (ebook) | ISBN 9781098281021 (Read-to-Me ebook)
Subjects: LCSH: Telephone--History--Juvenile literature. | Inventions--Juvenile literature. | Communication--History--Juvenile literature. | Inventions--History--Juvenile literature.
Classification: DDC 621.385--dc23

Table of Contents

Telephone

The invention of the telephone provided a fast and easy way to communicate. Scottish-born inventor Alexander Graham Bell gets most of the **credit** for coming up with the telephone.

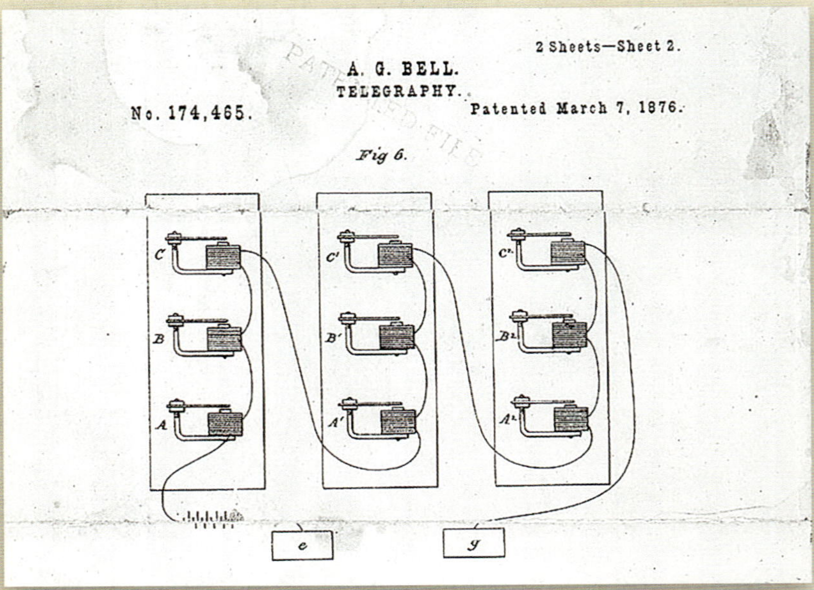

Bell first set out to make improvements to the **telegraph**. This led to the invention of the telephone.

Bell's box telephone

Bell received a **patent** for his invention on March 7, 1876. Three days later Bell and his assistant Thomas Watson spoke over the telephone for the first time.

movie reenactment

The first words were, "Mr. Watson, come here, I want to see you." The box telephone went on sale to the public in 1877.

How Did It Work?

Bell used a funnel to direct sound, or a voice, at a **membrane** on a machine. The sound made the membrane vibrate. This vibration created electrical signals.

12

The signals traveled along a wire to a receiver. Then the electrical signals were **converted** back to sounds.

Telephones today work like they did 150 years ago. The transmitter in the phone is like a microphone. It changes your voice into electrical signals. The other telephone receiver gets the signals. It then changes the signals back into sounds.

Landline signals travel on telephone wires. Wireless phone signals travel using radio waves. These waves bounce off a network of cellular towers.

Changes Over the Years

The telephone has changed and improved over the years. Telephones once had dials and later had push buttons. They were connected to a cord in the wall for power. Then, cell phones became popular.

Today, most people use smart phones. These are like small computers. Smart phones can make calls, take pictures, play music, and even track fitness!

More Facts

- The word telephone comes from two Greek words. *Tele* meaning "far" and *phone* meaning "voice."

- Bell experimented with sound when he was young. His mother was deaf and he looked for ways to communicate with her.

- The string telephone was created in 1667. The string carried sounds between two cans.

Glossary

converted – changed into another form or state.

credit – approval or praise given to a person for something that has been done.

landline – a telephone that is connected to the public network by a wire cable, or a telephone service connected by such cables.

membrane – a thin, soft pliable sheet or layer.

patent – a government grant that gives one the right to make, use, or sell an invention.

telegraph – a machine that puts messages in code and sends them along wires.

Index

Online Resources

Booklinks
NONFICTION NETWORK
FREE! ONLINE NONFICTION RESOURCES

To learn more about telephones, please visit **abdobooklinks.com** or scan this QR code. These links are routinely monitored and updated to provide the most current information available.